CORPORATE CONVICT

HOW TO NAVIGATE A SIX FIGURE CAREER
IN CORPORATE AMERICA

ERNEST R. MOSS

Corporate Convict

Copyright © 2022

Ernest R. Moss

All rights reserved

First Edition

DISCLAIMER

The advice contained in this material might not be suitable for everyone. The author designed the information to present his opinion about the subject matter. The reader must carefully investigate all aspects of any business decision before committing him or herself. The author obtained the information contained herein form sources he believes to be reliable and from his own personal experience, but he neither implies nor intends any guarantee of accuracy. The author is not in the business of giving legal, accounting, or any other type of professional advice. Should the reader need such advice, he or she must seek services from a competent professional. The author particularly disclaims any liability, loss, or risk taken by individuals who directly or indirectly act on the information contained herein. The author believes the advice presented here is sound, but readers cannot hold him responsible for either the actions they take, or the risk taken by individuals who directly or indirectly act on the information contained herein

DEDICATION

I want to dedicate this book to my momma, Cheryl Maw Moss. You were not here to see your oldest publish his first book, but you were always there for me through it all. Many have come and gone through this journey, but you held me down until God called you home. Love you, momma.

ACKNOWLEDGMENT

To my wife: Krissy, you have shown me what love and life is all about: NEMAL; my daughter: Mycala, my baby girl, we been through it, but we always remain, and the love never changes; my sons: Rara, Ernest Jr, Yaya, and Mish, thanks for putting up with my mood swings and distance. Pops had to get things flowing for the family; and all my young men: Ray 3rd, Donovan, Rayvon, and Jordan, thank you for being such a huge part of my growth as a man. Without my loved ones, I would not be the person I am today. Auntie, you have been my go-to person whenever times got tough. I'm here for you now.

To my P2P team, thank you for your dedication and for helping me spread my story to those who need some inspiration. I truly appreciate all that you do! And to all my corporate family and friends, those who have supported this change, encouraged me when I was feeling low and kicked my arse when my mind started to wonder, and doubt creeped up. Thanks for being an important part of my vision. Without you, no one knows where this wreck would   be

PREFACE

Damn, I wish I could start a new career, but I have things in my past and background that will make it difficult or damn near impossible. This book is a testimony to anyone who desires a career in corporate America and strategies and techniques to speed up the process and some of the pitfalls you can avoid on your path to greatness. This success story describes the strategic nature of an ex-con who had a desire to make six figures and show the world what he could do while on parole with everything designed to work against him. The same principles can apply to anyone who desires to start a successful career in corporate America. I can't speak for other industries, but I have navigated shark-infested waters in the corporate world and made a lot of money doing it. You can, too!

"If you believe, then you can achieve. Just look at me." -Tupac Shakur

CHAPTERS

INTRODUCTION

Ok, here we go again. This is the last time that I'm within these walls. "GOD HAS HIS HANDS ON ME. I WILL NOT FAIL." I never stopped uttering this statement. BELIEF is the first step to achieving whatever you desire, no matter the circumstances. I always remember that on my worse days, I live better than some on their best days. So, stop complaining.

My circumstances are not the best, to say the least. I am a three-time felon, and after serving the last 22 months in prison, I have:

- a GED, which I have had for 15 years
- two biological children—12 and 2 years of age—that depend on me
- a mom who's sick with cancer
- a family of drug addiction and crime
- seven years of parole before I finish this penal system for good

As I stated, to say the least. I could keep going about all the messed-up stuff that explains and defines my circumstances, but none of that even matters. I know that I am great and that I am going to do great things. I've felt this way my entire life. Through all the disappointments and losses, that feeling never left my belly. There's something greater for me. I just needed to figure it out. This isn't my first time getting out of prison, but it will be the last time. The first time, I was a lost kid who grew up in prison and came out without a plan. I was still hanging with knuckleheads that didn't mean the world any good, priding myself on street cred and keeping it real. I was giving myself and my energies to a group from yesterday, and it landed me back in prison. My plan doesn't involve any of them this time, so why even speak on it? Today, my words are only positive and full of energy. As I impatiently wait for my ride from this prison, I smile at the greatness that awaits me in the free world. The journey I envisioned each day while I was stuck in this place. Big Kool-Aid smile today! (While being pissed that they are not on time to pick me up!)

I've been preparing for this next chapter my entire time in prison. I felt like a failure and had to change my lifestyle because this was not the place to be.

The first step was my BELIEF system. Before you can achieve anything, you must believe that you can. I once believed that I could play in the NBA, but the reality was that I wasn't athletic like I thought I was and didn't have the work ethic, so I stopped believing in that. I once believed that I was smarter than the police. Well, as you can tell, I stopped believing in that too. The point is that I had to be REALISTIC with my abilities to achieve this greatness, and the NBA just wasn't it, nor was trying to outsmart the police. Yes, many will challenge that statement, and they have that right. But I accepted that reality and adjusted my belief system. You can hold on to your NBA dreams and gangster mindset and let me know how that works for you. I am excited about my next chapter, and I believe I have greatness within me. I plan to do something to make my mom and my kids proud of me. I believe that.

Ok, so now I believe. What's next? A brainstorming session fueled by RESEARCH; step 2. I hit the law library and started looking for books on success and what it takes to be rich. The guys looked at me as if I had lost my mind overnight. Up to this point, my readings were from Donald Goines and Dean Koontz, authors that allowed you to live within the prison walls in fantasy and kill time. My first success-focused book was *Rich Dad, Poor Dad*. If you haven't read this book, you should. It changed my entire outlook on life and finances. He stated that savers are losers. I thought, wow, I need to read this book because I wasn't raised to believe that. The focus was on investing over saving. This is what the rich teach their children. I'd never been around any rich people, so I wanted to know what they were teaching. While a good read, I was still searching for my niche or product that would become my new career. I just knew that I would be at six figures within five years of my release. I didn't have a backup plan. This was it.

I needed to change some of my habits while educating myself. I stopped watching SportsCenter every day and started watching the news instead. The news can be very depressing, so ensure you focus on why you are watching. I wanted to know what was trending, what the highest paying salaries were, and more importantly, which of these companies would hire a three-time felon. I prayed for clarity, and as it often happens in my life, it was revealed to me during a chess game—something I'm very good at, by the way. My opponent heard my passion for change during several games and enlightened me on the fact that the prison I was at had a computer class, and he would participate in the next session. I thought, well, I know nothing about computers. "Good luck, my brother. I hope you get some good stuff out of the class." We continued to play chess, but that stuck in my brain. Computers.

He asked me what my plans were and where I saw myself in five years. It didn't require much thought. I told him I saw myself in a tailored suit, carrying a leather briefcase and telling my assistant to hold all calls as I sat in my big leather chair in front of my desk, making six figures. Everybody within ear range laughed or told me I was crazy as hell. I just smiled. They obviously don't know who I am, I said to myself. Yeah, I had won the chess tournament and was a badass, but wasn't I smart enough to pull that dream off? I continued to smile because the doubt motivated me even more. I'm an Aries, and we love challenges. He further said I should investigate the computer class. The world is going digital anyway, so why not find out what it's about? In prison, you have plenty of time to investigate new things. You know what, I just might do that, I thought. The only thing I knew about computers from my short time out was how to get popups and viruses. I was still trying to get used to a cellular phone and all that it did, but I was intrigued.

The very next day, I did some research on a career in computer science or information technology. Again, something I had no clue about. But the prison had a program here, and I had about a year left until my parole date, so it was worth the research. As I started researching information technology, I learned that in this field, it's more about what you know and not about what your background shows. All different races and cultures are part of technology. And the salaries can reach six figures within a few years. SOLD! I signed up for the next computer class. I also started to teach myself how to type with the Mavis Beacon program. I remember my big clumsy hands messing up. I started out typing 12 good words a minute. For those that know, that's horrible! I would go to that library and practice a lot! Friends would ask me about playing dominoes or cards, but I was locked in. You need to learn how to type. *This is an essential tool for your success in corporate America.* I couldn't wait for this computer class to start. I had found my new career, and I was all in. Yes, it requires some math, so if you plan to go on the information technology career path, brush up on your math. *There are a lot of free courses online that can help with that.* That was easy for me.

Step 3: Daily Habits. Through my research, I wanted to know what an IT (information technology) career looked like; what they wore, how they looked, what schools they went to, and so on. I mainly found nerdy-looking people or Indians. So I thought, 'what can I do to fit into this crowd? I have always been a decent-looking guy. What could I do to look like a professional?' The next day, I shaved all my facial hair and got a haircut. Yeah, the fellas got off their jokes at my expense, but I was on a mission, and their laughter only motivated me. I started to study proper etiquette and mannerisms that were professional-focused. I started paying attention to shows with professional information technology actors, just to see their mannerisms. I finished with the *Rich Dad, Poor Dad* book and started reading *The 7 Habits of Highly Effective People.* Another great read, if you haven't already. Ok, so I changed my appearance, started watching the news as a daily habit, and read a book for no less than an hour a day—normally, more. What else could I do while confined to this prison dump? I just felt like I wasn't doing enough. *Taking on a lot of change at once can be rough, so ease into it if you feel it's too much. Be consistent with the things you change as you grow; you'll continue to change.*

Step 4: Words. All the religious, philosophical, and success books have something in common; Words mean stuff. There's a power in our words. What you consistently say and listen to has power in your life. Good or bad. I was raised with the saying, "Sticks and stones may break my bones, but words will never hurt me." That's an outright lie! Words can hurt far more than a physical injury. You would understand if you have been hurt by what someone said. Years later, it could still hurt. While that broken bone is healed, your heart will never be the same. Words are essential to success. Positive affirmations daily will help form and strengthen your belief system. Constantly remind yourself that you are GREAT. Say it like Tony the Tiger used to say it; GREEEEAAAATTTTTTTTT! While saying that you are great, you cannot sound as if you are dumb. Cussing or being loud is not how professionals speak unless they are entertainers. I wasn't.

My vocabulary was limited to street slang. Instead of reading past words and hoping the author would explain so that they made sense, I started to look up their meaning. I stopped using so much profanity. Not everyone appreciates profanity, especially around their loved ones. It makes sense to me; talk like someone who is about to get a degree and make six figures a year. I noticed something immediately; many of my fellow prison mates who used to love to sit around and talk shit suddenly didn't invite me into the cipher of shit talking, like before. Look at the power of the WORD. As soon as I started talking properly and about being successful, my crowd moved and decreased in numbers. Now my greetings went from, "What up Mf?" to "All shit, here comes this proper college Mf." I thought it was a joke and just a witty statement but let's just say our conversations decreased, and my reading increased. Win-win.

Before we move on from this step, I want you to pay attention to the words you say and the conversations you have. Are they success focused? Are they positive in nature? If the answer to this is no, start changing your words. We can control what others say by being consistent with what we say and what we entertain. Listening to someone complain all the time or talk doom and gloom about life will not aid you during this journey. That is their default, so they will not change their conversation, but they will change how often they bring it to you. Have no fear. They'll find someone else to drop their sorrows on, just not you. We all have 24 hours in a day. What you choose to do with yours is up to you. Be prepared for the change because, if being successful is what you desire, it should be displayed through your words, acts, and deeds. Everything and everybody will start to change around you.

Finally, Step 5; Plan. Ideas are great, and thoughts come and go. Document your plan. It doesn't have to be written in stone but needs to be documented. Record it if you can't write and listen to it daily. Read your plan DAILY. Out loud. Make sure that it makes sense to you. Your peers may ridicule you for it, but you believe in it, and that's what matters. Yeah, you can say, "My plan is to be rich," but without steps to achieve your plan, it's just an idea or thought. An idle mind can think of some wild stuff. Make your plan actionable. Break it down into steps or goals. These should all roll up to the ultimate goal. Put a timebox around some of these, if you can. Just saying that you want to live a long time isn't going to prepare you to live a long time. Google SMART goals.

My plan includes attending college and changing my lifestyle to fit into this new IT world. Many successful people did not go to college, and I get it. Two things can be true; I only have a GED, and I know I need some credentials behind my name. I filed for my FAFSA (Free Application for Federal Student Aid) at the law library. I was so clueless about what I needed to do that it drove me to continue doing my research.

I needed to find a college near my home that would accept a GED. What better school to start with technology, ITT Technical Institute? We've all seen the commercials. Everyone looks like they are living a pretty good life to me. I applied while still in prison, and my plan is to start with the September 07 class. Today is June 22, 2007. I completed the computer course, and the next step is to start college.

Let's recap.

- Belief. Without this, we are just looking at pies in the sky. If you don't believe in yourself, it will be very hard, if not impossible, to achieve the greatness that you have within you. We all have something to offer the world.

- Brainstorm through research. I was taught that when you fail to research, you forfeit your right to speak on something. Do your research, align with your beliefs, and find your niche. This doesn't happen overnight, and you will be required to put in that work. You may discover that you don't want to do what you set out to do. That's ok. Find something else that fits your goals.

- Adjust your daily habits. Humans are habitual by nature. Because of years of programming through multiple avenues, we do things without thinking about what we are doing—upbringing, media, social norms, and so on. You cannot expect to be wealthy if you have poor habits. Poor isn't just a matter of money or things; it's a MINDSET. Most of our minds have been set by how we were raised. We need to brainwash! That filthy thing has collected enough bullshit over the years. It needs washing. Suds that thing up, rinse and repeat as needed.

- Words. I repeat, there's a power in the word. No one knows what you are thinking, but they know what you are speaking, and you will be judged by that. Speak your riches into existence. Everyone in your circle should know what they can and can't say to you, and the easiest way for them to know is by the words that come out of your mouth.

- Plan. This is the final step to achieving success. You must have a plan! Some may say they don't need a plan and will just figure it out. And you can, but it will be much easier to throw you off, or life happens. Have you an actionable plan? Document it and read it often. Yes, plans can change and often do, but they have a starting point, which is what I want you to do; create a plan and build upon it.

These steps were started while I was in prison. Maybe you've never been incarcerated within prison walls. I hope that you haven't and wouldn't. Either way, ask yourself now, are you a prisoner of your past choices, upbringing, or financial situation? Maybe it's your thoughts that imprison you and limit your success. Nevertheless, it's time to break down those walls and remove the excuses. Excuses are toxic to success. Excuses should be given no words or energy during this transformation. They were created for your past life. Let's leave that there and change what we THINK is successful. This is part of my story; no, this is not a prison story, and the habits that I created and principles that I live by can be applied to any situation. Whether you have been incarcerated physically, emotionally, or mentally, this book can assist you with your journey to riches. But hey, my ride is finally here, and although late, nothing can upset me today. I'm going home to my family and loved ones.

Chapter 1
Reentry

For those of you reading or listening to this, there are no words that can explain how it feels to be released from prison. This is not a story about prison. This is a success story. A story about how you can start a new career with no experience. I was finally free after 22 months, and I had my GED and a plan to be great. This 'big plan' is common for most that are released back into society. The problem is that most don't follow through with their plan and get involved with what they know best—crime. Even the guards laugh and say on your way out, "You'll be back like the rest of them." My response was, "We shall see." Statistics will say that they are right. "Within three years of release, 67.8% of ex-offenders are rearrested, and within five years,76.6% are rearrested." These were the percentages when this book was written. I've seen it and experienced it. There comes a time when you just get tired of the bullshit, tired of failing and starting over. I will not remain a statistic. I know that I am better than anything that I have been through. Just knowing it or saying it means nothing. Actions speak louder than words, but words still mean stuff. So, be careful of what you say and who you say it around. You may think that everyone has your back and wants what's best for you, and then you may realize that it's not that black and white. Salt and sugar look the same until you taste them, so keep your eyes on the prize and embrace the change.

I was greeted with all the love and energy from my family and friends while being excited and nervous, and it felt great! I was also greeted with the fact that the bills were in bad shape, and I needed to get a job to lighten the load my spouse had been carrying for 22 months while I was in prison. College was still three months away, and my parole officer was not trying to hear that I was waiting for my first class; I was stipulated to get a job. Three-time felon with a GED and a plan to be at six figures within five years? Even my momma laughed at me when I started working at Burger King. My pride and ego were on full display, but I needed to do whatever I could to help my family get out of the red I had caused. That $9 an hour was all the help I could provide, but it did help a little. All I wanted to do was help with the bills and get this PO off my back because I didn't have a job—done.

Homelife was tough. I had left my family to deal with the world without me, and there was some bitterness from all angles. My teenage daughter was developing into a woman, and my 2-year-old seemed afraid of me, which hurt. I was different than when I went in, and everyone felt that change. I explained my plan, and the family was supportive while being skeptical. Fair enough, I'll show you all. Each day, I did research. I had a computer in the palms of my hands. My IT career was around the corner as I flipped burgers with teenagers and humbled myself. I didn't need anyone's belief in me. I could conquer the world on my own. That was a mistake that eventually cost me my family and marriage. I was withdrawn while being focused on my plan. I couldn't help my family without pursuing my goals and creating a new career. All they wanted was time, and my time was limited.

12

Old friends would pop up often to kick the shit and reminisce about some of the crazy stuff we had done. All I wanted to talk about was college and changing my career to reach my number; 6-figures. That brought about many laughs and 'yeah rights.' No one was interested in listening to a convict, fresh out of prison, talking about making six figures with three felonies and a GED, working at Burger King. I even went to the Plasma Center and donated blood to get a few dollars in my pocket. The talk was all about life and how messed up it was. "The system is designed to keep us down," "The white man won't allow us to be great," "It's hard to get a job with these felons," "my baby momma did this." I was so tired of hearing the complaints and excuses. Many of these so-called friends were becoming less relevant in my life. I needed to find like-minded people. Everyone I knew was poverty-stricken, and that's all they wanted to talk about. It became depressing to be around certain people because it was the same story each time. *This is where WORDS become impactful. If you constantly allow yourself to remain in these circles, with negative conversations being the focal point of the circle, negativity will remain a part of you. It's the crabs in the bucket mentality.* So, many in my circle had accepted their fate and found comfort in simplicity. I wanted so much more. I was like, "Damn, I have enough mess to think about. Let's talk about something else." Even then, the conversations would find a way to hit a negative tone, and I knew then that I needed a new circle—time to brainstorm and step up my RESEARCH.

Chapter 2
New Circle

How do I find a new circle? Will I fit in? Who do the IT professionals hang out with? Where do they hang out? They are damn sure not in the hood, where I often find myself. I'm a hood dude, and yeah, I found comfort there—until I didn't. They were also not hanging out at a burger place, so how could I get in? College was getting closer, yet my surroundings were the same as when I went to prison. I learned how to use Google on my cell phone and searched 'Hangouts for IT Professionals.' You'll be surprised at what you will find. I was shocked at the number of meet-ups and networking events. I was excited as hell to attend my first event and get to know some like-minded people. Then it dawned on me; I had no professional clothes.

My wardrobe consisted of a few pairs of jeans and a couple of polo shirts. That may not be the best thing to wear to a networking event unless you plan on sweeping the floor. I needed to step up my gear game, but money was limited. I humbled myself and went to the Goodwill. I'm 6'2" and 275 lbs, so it's difficult to buy off the rack, much less pick through used clothes. But hey, here we are. The beauty in all of this is that I found a pair of pants and a button-up shirt. Not the best, but it served the purpose. I know that clothes do not make a person, but let's be honest, we all judge based on clothing. It's a defense mechanism. For example, if you see a large bald-headed man with many tattoos walking toward you, your initial thought is different

14

compared to someone in a suit and tie. Both, or neither, could be dangerous, but our built-in defense mechanism kicks in, and you wonder, is this big, tatted guy going to try to rob me? Is this person in this suit coming to lock me up? Maybe they work at a bank. It doesn't matter. You still judged that person by their appearance. We all do. And the skin and suit were contrasting examples. Is it fair? Nope, and neither is life. Get that out of your head. 'Fair' is a place where they judge pigs. It doesn't exist in real life. So, you may see someone expressing themselves, wearing revealing clothes, showing off tattoos, and so on, and they are very successful. The difference is that they may not have the felonies you have or the situation you are trying to change. Their parents may have helped them to become successful. Who cares? You shouldn't because this is about you and what you can do and must do to be successful. If you have a lack mindset, you will do and get what your hand calls for. You can become complacent if you continue to measure yourself against those in similar situations and circumstances. *Measure yourself against the wealthy and successful, and then see if you measure up. Stay motivated.*

I was nervous as hell! Just walking through the door caused my stomach to cramp. My first networking event was one of the most difficult things I've done. I knew no one, and I thought everyone in the room could see that I was an ex-con. Paranoid, to say the least, but I was there. What I will say is that they treated me kindly. I've never been one to be shy when speaking, so I started to mingle, and everyone was supportive of my new career move and offered advice. I took it all. I took notes the entire time I was there, and some found that impressive. If I could fit into this crowd with used clothes and a smile, I could only imagine how it would be when I brought something to the conversation besides a career move. Some of the things they talked about were like a foreign language to me, but I nodded, smiled, and continued to take notes. I had found my circle. I live by the metaphor, "Birds of a feather flock together. Ducks don't fly with Eagles." It was time to fly high and spread these Eagle wings.

This is part of your daily habits. You can't expect to be successful if you surround yourself with, and get your advice from, unsuccessful people. Our parents may have advice, but you must remember that the world has changed since they started their careers. It doesn't matter if it is a successful family member. If they are not trying to better their lives, you need to remove yourself from that circle and change your daily habits. They may mean well, but their thoughts and principles are not conducive to what you are doing.

Dare to do wondrous things. Try new things that you have never thought of doing. Pick an evening or a time, look up 'networking events near me,' and go to one. It doesn't have to be related to your field of choice. Just go to one and mingle with the people. Learn how to talk to strangers. You are on a journey where you have never been, so it's going to feel weird, and you may feel hesitant. Swallow those fears and go with your goal in mind. This is the most important; tell yourself out loud what your goal is and put a number with it; "My Goal will allow me to make a salary of…." There's power in the word and when you put this in the atmosphere, watch how your baby starts to form, how your crop will start yielding you a harvest as you've never believed. It'll only work if you truly believe that it will. Society, friends, and family will throw things your way to test your belief. As you stand firm, they'll adjust. They have no choice because we are on to greater things. You may discover that everyone you thought had your back and best interest at heart can be the same ones who do everything they can to persuade you to do something else. You may have to guard your goals from your momma. Give them time. They'll see you in action and then wonder how you did it.

I want to make sure that I highlight this area. Up to this point, we have focused on everyone except you. You must lead with your vision, your goals, and your beliefs. If you complain as much as the others, then you will be placed into that bucket. Reputation goes a long way with a new career. Yes, times will most likely get rough, and yes, you will have some setbacks, but complaining about it to whoever will listen will not serve you. Friends and family will say, "See, I told you. That's just how life works." Blah blah blah. Don't feed yourself with this mess. Life will give you what you desire. Is your belief stronger than an obstacle? It better be, or you will fail.

Chapter 3
First Day of College

Here we go. It's time to put this plan into action! "After doing years in prison, this is a piece of cake," I told myself. It wasn't. The networking event was a piece of cake compared to starting at a college with an old GED, and again, I knew no one. It's not strange that I didn't know anyone because outside of the networking event, my circle was the have-nots, so I expected that. *Fear has no place in what I plan to do.* I sat alone in the break room and simply observed my classmates. Most, if not all, were there alone, with no one they knew. So, I found peace in that. Plus, they were dressed no better than I was, and all my clothes were from hood stores. My car was about the oldest in the parking lot, and my driver-side window didn't roll down, but it got me here, which is important. The finer things in life will come. Until then, I'll keep buying from the $1 menu. *Trust the process.*

I immediately noticed that I was among the oldest and often the oldest in my classes. Most of my classmates were fresh out of high school. They knew more about computers than I had ever imagined. My computer class in prison barely scratched the surface of what I needed to know to be successful. The instructors were saying terms that I had no clue about, and yes, I felt intimidated. I wasn't used to being in a circle where I was the least knowledgeable. So, I started studying like a mad man. I sat in the front row of every class and raised my hand often if it was something that I didn't understand. I was paying for this education, and they were going to teach me. I thought some of my questions showed my true ignorance, but I asked anyway. I wasn't concerned with any of my classmates. Hell, I knew no one still. I started to come early on the days I had a class or had to study, and a few of my classmates were there too. So, I approached a couple of guys and just asked about what they were studying. From there, we grew friendships. We are still friends to this day. I had added to my new circle. After we took finals, we would hang out at the end of each quarter at B Dubs (Buffalo Wild Wings).

Now, I must describe these additions to my new circle. For starters, I was the oldest. Only one other guy had children, and they were babies. I was the only convicted felon and the only person who had been to jail. But I never let them know that, and they still don't know unless they are reading this book right now. This was by design because I didn't want to be judged by my past or looked at differently. I was just an old college dude starting a new career. I wanted to be the new me, and they accepted me with open arms. We used to compete to see who would get the best grades or miss the most days. When we had group projects, we always tried to team up. Everyone in my circle had straight A's, so you had to come with it. They pushed me to study much harder to keep up with them, who had been raised with computers. Yeah, I laughed at some of their old man jokes, and hell, I was only 32. *Control your sensitive nature. We walk through life with our guards up when we don't have to. Sometimes we do, but in a college setting, it's not required.*

I met someone in one of my general education classes. With general education, you can find yourself in a class with people from all walks of life. Not just IT. This young lady was not in IT. She was part of the criminal justice program and wanted to be a police officer. Why did they have to match the only convict in the room with the police? My prison defense mechanism kicked in, and I was distant to start, but she wouldn't allow that. Nor would I allow her slacking to cause me to get anything below an A, so we became cool. She started calling me 'Unc' because, again, I was often the oldest in the class. To this day, we are close. Closer than most. I'm still 'Unc,' and she's 'Niecy.' I could write a book on what she and I have been through, but I won't, for now. However, I will say that the same person I was hesitant to speak to was the same person who allowed me to sleep on her couch when I was homeless, the same person who introduced me to millionaires and started me on my journey to finer things. I've had the opportunity to speak at some of her events, and we even passed out food to the homeless. I love her, her family, and moreover, her passion for greatness. Yeah, she's still wild and crazy, but hey, so am I. *You may never know who could help take your life to the next level, so treat everyone with respect and as you would like to be treated. Remember that you are starting over, and with that will come people that have nothing in common with you but could change your life. Stay open and receptive to assistance. You don't have to walk alone.*

I had a new circle, and the instructors knew exactly who I was because it was impossible not to notice the student that kept his hand up. I applied for a position at the school as a student worker. It only paid $9 an hour, but I thought if I was spending so much time at the school, why not get paid for it? The Dean called me into his office after running a background check on me. He shook his head and turned me down for the job. My background was too bad, and he even asked me to consider changing my degree because it would be hard to find someone to hire me. I'll never forget the look of concern on that man's face when I smiled and said, "God has His Hands on me. I cannot fail." He passed from cancer and couldn't experience my success, but I'll never forget that look he gave me and the smile I gave him. *Had I not been firm in my belief, that conversation could have rattled me and caused negative thoughts to arise, but it didn't. That was his fear speaking, and while he may have meant good, I brushed it off and kept it moving.* A funny thing happened. The school had a new administration, and I had become friends with one of the instructors who took a leadership position, vouched for me, and allowed me to become a student worker, even with my background.

Remember this: People will tell you, "No," "Stop," and "Don't." I say, "No, don't stop." Life, friends and family, bills, and spouses will have their opinion about what you should or shouldn't do. My advice: get counsel from successful people who have navigated the waters you are in. Do some research and find a mentor or a coach.

They could come with a price tag, and if they are good, they will, and that's ok. Their knowledge of your field could be valued at a few hundred or several thousand dollars. Pay it and get that knowledge. Millionaires have mentors and coaches. One of the ways that the rich continue to get richer.

Success likes speed, and I like speed. I like the fast track to achieving my goals. A mentor or coach can and will help with that. I've had several mentors and coaches throughout this journey. They will become part of your team and new circle. Listen to the instructions that they give! If you had all of the answers you would be their mentor but you're not.

Chapter 4
Sensei

The parole board stipulated that I do anger management, and I had put it off for as long as I could. I didn't feel I needed any of this program mess, so I came through the door with the RBF (resting bitch face). The leader of the program was a gentleman that they called Sensei. A Billy Blanks-looking dude with a shit-eating grin (Thank Maw for this saying. I might tell you about it one day). My mean looks made him laugh to the point that I started laughing. This man has a laugh that will stop you in your tracks! I began to enjoy attending his class and realized I had more anger and resentment in me than I thought. All the past pains and mistakes were weighing heavy on my conscious, and I didn't know this before this class. What I did notice was that they had a room with computers, so I was intrigued. They were not doing much with them because they were outdated and low-quality. I volunteered to work in their computer lab if I could complete this program and get this parole officer off my back. Plus, I could add to my resume that I had a position as a technical lead for their reentry/anger management program. Win, win. I would work in that computer lab and study at the same time. I was helping prisoners who were just out of prison with resumes and cover letters. Some started with the same typing program that I had when I was in prison. A couple applied for college and did great things with that little guidance I gave them. What was weird was that I had only been out for a few months, and here I was, teaching a class that I was still in the process of learning. *Every so often, I will run into one of my students, and it feels good to know they— not all but some—are still on the path to greatness.*

I started to do martial arts with Sensei. I thought I was pretty good at fighting, but he humbled me quickly. This old man was dangerous with some of the things he could do. He used his martial arts techniques for anger management, which worked. I learned how to breathe properly and how to meditate. Not to mention, I learned some defense tactics and started to lose weight. He became not just my Sensei, but he became a spiritual advisor. My go-to person when life was kicking my ass and I wanted to scream out. He would listen to my complaints and cries and would laugh at me. It pissed me off all the time, but that was the clue that this was nothing. He kept me focused on my goal and always reminded me that on my worst days, I live like some on their best. So, stop allowing life to give me excuses. His favorite phrase is, 'Excuses are like buttholes. Some stink more than others." They all stink, so don't allow yourself to focus on the excuses because they will be there.

My advice? We should all seek counseling or therapy, one-on-one or in groups. It can only be helpful and while I know that we don't need that and there's nothing wrong with us, find someone. Find someone neutral who will not judge you based on your past. Your spiritual well-being is critical to your success. Its great that many of us belong to churches, clubs, groups, and religious organizations that provide support. Find what works for you and consider investing in yourself for that one-to-one conversation with a person who is not judging you. We don't know them anyway. Do your research, and you will find a lot of programs out there that are free and resourceful. Trying to do this alone can cause you a lot of unnecessary suffering. I know because I sacrificed everything for my success, and I didn't have to. Build your circle, your team, and keep a therapist on speed dial. Meditate more. There are lessons online that will guide you if you don't know how to meditate. My favorite meditation is to close my eyes and envision myself at my forever home with the breeze flowing and the smell of the ocean in my nostrils. You must picture your reward for this work, or it can remain a mystery. Close your eyes and see it! I find my peace in appreciating what I have and excitement in knowing what I have coming.

Chapter 5
Time to Step Up

My classes were going great. Homelife, not so much. My family wanted me to spend more time at home because they missed me, and I missed them. I was working two part-time jobs and going to school full-time. I was so hungry for success that I overlooked their concerns, something I have had to live with. I can't say I would do anything differently if I had a chance to do it all again. I saw my path to six figures, and I was not going to slow down or pause for anyone, not even my family. That could sound harsh, but my rationale was that I was no good to my family if I couldn't provide and ended up back in prison. The entire house was becoming distant, and my daughter was starting to act out. My son was born premature and had constant visits from therapists and doctors. I missed most of those because of my schedule. I wanted to be a great dad to them, but I was doing a bad job at it. I just thought it would all be better once I was in my career and could provide them with a better life. So, I kept spending my time at school, between jobs. I had started a new career that was nothing I had ever done, but it was fun and life changing.

I couldn't keep flipping burgers, and my school schedule didn't align with my hours, so I put in my two-week notice and started looking for another job. I didn't care what my parole officer said because she couldn't say anything if I was a full-time student and paid my $30 a month. I enjoyed bringing her my grades, and they were all A's. I found a part-time job working for a catering company. It was easy work compared to the hard labor I was used to, and I got to wear nice clothes. So I stepped my gear game up and became great at the job.

One of their sister companies kept getting robbed. Everyone in this coffee shop was small framed, young, with blonde hair, and there was one woman whom I love as a sister to this day; Karen, aka Juicy. Juicy taught me how to run that coffee shop. My only request when I accepted that job was that I had to be able to study when things were slow. College came first over everything. They agreed. I really loved that coffee shop. I met so many professional people and had many conversations with strangers. It allowed me to come out of that *reserved shell* naturally developed by people with my background. Using my WORDS, some of those strangers are friends to this day. You may be tired of me saying that line, but I mean it. To this day, none of them know that I have a background. I didn't wear that on my sleeve because, like my circle at school, I wanted them to see the new me. I was developing a new circle that wasn't focused on grades and college. These were just regular people, and I loved that. Oh, and the coffee shop never got robbed under my watch.

The coffee shop was in the Visitor Center in Forest Park. Often, I had to sit at the front desk after I had clocked out of the coffee shop. The visitor center workers were often late to their shifts, so they didn't mind me studying at the rotunda, and I was ok with it. Plus, I had time to kill before my classes started. And I liked talking to the visitors who would come in from all over the world and wanted to know about St Louis. Being strategic, I applied for a position at the visitor center, and because they knew me, I didn't have to interview. They gave me that job, which I accepted. I went from one job to the next, and they were both in the same building. Neither job paid much. I made more from tips in the coffee shop than my hourly rate, but the experience was priceless and added another slot to my resume.

The great people that I met while working there will never be forgotten. I even met a celebrity who saw me studying at the rotunda and asked what I was studying. We talked briefly, and I found something funny about this guy. Like I knew him from somewhere. I told him that he looked familiar, and he started to smile. I couldn't put my finger on it, but I had seen him before. Long story short, he stated that he was an actor and had been on the Cosby Show. I said, "COCKROACH!" He said nope and laughed because no one had ever called him a cockroach. He was the young doctor that delivered the baby when Bill couldn't do it. He had also played Preacher Man on The Five heartbeats. Nothing came of that; I just thought that it was dope that I had been holding a conversation with a celebrity about my studies and my goals. *Everyone in your circle and that you encounter should know your goal. Don't be bashful about it. That shows a lack of belief. No, I'm not saying the guy at the drive-through window needs to know your goals, but if someone comes into your life, there is a reason.* When you lead with your goals, it will run those who mean you no good away and draw those who do mean you good closer. Bad energy hates to be around good energy. Try it. Meet with one of your friends or family members who are not doing their best or struggling, and start talking about how great you plan to be and

28

what your goals are. Their response will be to change the subject, or they had to go because something just came up.

I wanted business cards to highlight my career change. I went to Vistaprint and ordered a bundle. Everyone that I knew had computer issues. Mainly viruses and adware, but I knew how to clean them up. I could do a few quick tricks to speed up most computers. I didn't charge much. I hoped to get a tank of gas for my time. I was still in hustle mode, so it seemed like the best thing to do. Why not put what I was learning to practice? The school did a hardware refresh. This means that they were replacing all the computers at the school and had a lot of bad computers. The dean knew what my side hustle was and asked me if I could make 12 old computers disappear. Of course, I could.

I had to replace some drives and RAM and add new software—software I was given through the school as a student. When I finished those 12 computers, I had 10 great ones for sale. It took me only a couple of weeks to get the school's trash to work properly. I sold each of those for $100 a pop. It didn't cost me more than $20, and I made $1000. The Dean could've gotten rid of all those computers, but he knew me and my ambition. The clients I helped with speeding up their computers bought each of my refurbished computers. I had so many referrals that I couldn't keep up with the demands. Some still contact me today about viruses on their computers. At this point, my free time was spent working on computers and trying to keep gas in my beater. I still had my old car, but it was reliable, and we rolled until I could purchase a better car.

Chapter 6
First Graduation

I completed my associate degree with straight A's. It was one of the proudest moments of my life because I never made it to high school, so I had never graduated with anything but my GED, and I was in juvenile detention when I did that. Walking across that stage does something to you. Hearing your family scream and cheer is priceless. I'd never given my mom anything to be proud of until now. She cried, and we both cried. Dying from cancer and barely able to walk around the place, she was happy that her eldest was doing something with his life. My family was the only ones in that arena who knew my story and that I had done this while on parole. This was my goal; to graduate with my associate's degree and get a job in IT.

My PLAN took a shift because now I wanted my bachelor's degree. I was taught that the higher your education level, the more money you could make. Plus, I had just done two years with straight A's. I had the momentum, and I kept going. This caused even more strain at home because everyone knew my PLAN, and now, I was changing it. And again, I won't be at home much. Nothing I said convinced my family that I was doing this for us and that this would be great soon. One thing led to another, and to make a long story short, I ended up divorced. I don't think my son has ever forgiven me for that, but you will have regrets in life. I had custody of my daughter, who was by another woman, so I had to find us somewhere to live.

A family member allowed my daughter to have a room in her basement. I would pick her up daily to take her to school because she didn't want to change high schools. I pretty much lived out of my car or on couches. I ate fast food from the $1 menu each day and would hope that something was left in the breakroom. It beat being in prison, so I kept my head high. This only lasted a month or so, and then I found us a townhouse that I could afford. Everything in that house was given to us by someone in the family because we had no furniture or anything for a home. But we had each other, and that's what mattered. Being a felon with no credit makes it very hard for someone to rent to you. I had a family member vouch for my daughter and me, and they bypassed the background and credit check and allowed us to move in. We had no furniture, no dishes, nothing. My family all rallied to our aid, and within days, we had a house full of furniture and cabinets full of non-matching dishes. But we had a place to stay with the necessities, and I had a home for my son and daughter— no more sleeping in cars and on other people's couches.

My daughter was 14, and she had to be the woman of the house. I robbed her of a lot of her childhood, but she loves me for everything I did to get to this point. She didn't understand at the time, and I couldn't convince her to hear me, but it feels good when she says, "Dad, you were right, and I just didn't want to listen to your strict rules back then." For those who are reading this and struggling with a home, get yourself a vehicle because it got me where I needed, and it was a home when I needed one. *Yes, your pride will kick in, but humble yourself and read your goal out loud. The end will justify the means, but you must stick to the plan. Remember where you've been and what you've been through. This obstacle is nothing but a bump on the road. Our ego or pride often directs our thoughts to take the wrong actions. Guard yourself against your old self.*

Chapter 7
REOS

My first IT job was for the nonprofit where I had to take my anger management class for the parole board. I was volunteering up to this point because I've always been passionate about giving back. I enjoyed helping those newly released with their resumes and cover letters and how to set up emails, and so on. Plus, this kept me sharp because I was studying on the job. Then the company bided on a large grant and got it. They had enough in the budget to pay me a salary. It wasn't much, but it did give me another new slot on my resume. I needed to build up my experience if I was going to get into corporate America. I accepted it and met with a friend of mine, Benny. This veteran had a presence about himself, and I was intrigued to know who he was. So, I simply knocked on his door, introduced myself to him, and told him my story and plans. He had the idea that I could be the first to speak to each group of newly released prisoners. Men and women. He saw me as a success story and someone they would listen to. I didn't agree with the success story partly because I hadn't reached my goal yet. But I didn't turn him down. I wanted everyone getting out of prison to have a chance to be successful. Me being out two years and making straight A's, with no violations, was a success story to them.

I took that thought and did what I could to touch some of them who were just getting out. I wanted to touch them all, but some had other plans. They saw me as another suit in front of them, telling them how to live. I'll never forget the looks on their face when they realized that while in this suit, I had been where they just came from, and I was doing pretty good for myself. I had been incarcerated with a few of them, but they didn't recognize me in a suit and clean, shaved face. As I stated, some listened, and some didn't. The program had its funding pulled after a few sessions, but it feels good when I run into some of that group, and they tell me how well they are doing and how I made them believe they could do it. That alone is enough to make you get up and shake whatever is bothering you. Some people are happy just to be free, yet we find ourselves complaining about the gas prices or the weather.

Chapter 8
1st IT Job in Corporate America

My bachelor's degree classes were easier than those of the associate's degree. I was a student worker at the visitor center and ran the coffee shop on weekends, still with straight A's and a little cockiness because now, I knew my stuff with computers. I was no longer the weak link in my group or circle. The teachers knew me on a first-name basis and would call on me in class to help with some of the dry subjects. There was a recruiting team on the school campus while I was working there, and many of the graduates or soon-to-be graduates were there to do mock interviews. I was just up there sweeping the floor and changing the trash in my student worker polo. One of the college recruiters thought it would be good practice for me to do a mock interview. I wasn't prepared because all the other students wore suits, ties, and dresses. I was in a dirty polo with 'ITT Tech' on it. Plus, I had never heard of Savvis. I had no clue what the company did, and I didn't have a resume to present to them, but I did the mock interview anyway. They loved me! They asked if I could do a technical interview with their engineers over the phone, and of course, I said yes. I hadn't graduated, so I didn't think I had a chance for this position. But it was good practice, so I was calm for the phone interview. I had applied at several companies with open IT positions and had rarely received a callback. My expectations were low. The questions they asked me were easy to begin, but then they started talking about things I had never heard of. I began to sweat under my arms. The pressure was growing, and I responded like anyone in this position would have; "I haven't studied that aspect of IT, but I am a student with straight A's, so wherever I need to focus, I can learn it." They called me for another interview, this time in person.

I started to believe that I could get this job in IT. Up to this point, I saw the interview as practice because I hadn't graduated with my bachelor's degree. But they called me back for another interview, so they must have liked something about me. I started to practice my interview skills. I would ask all the staff to do mock interviews with me. Part of the final interview was a 10-minute PowerPoint presentation about how my skills could help Savvis. One thing that you must be able to sell is yourself. I was pretty good at that because everyone in school loved me and had no clue that a felon was in their midst. I worked on that presentation every day and did mock interviews every day. The school counselors and career recruiters would turn the other way when they saw me coming with a smile on my face. I wouldn't accept no for an answer. It was their job to prepare me for this position, and I was going to ensure they did their job. I would do my interview in the mirror and watch my facial expressions to ensure I didn't answer with the RBF (resting bitch face). The closer the interview got, the more nervous I got. But it was time to pull up my bootstraps and make it happen. *"God has His Hands on me. I cannot fail."*

I had one of two suits that I owned dry cleaned. My presentation had been combed over by all the staff and some of my IT buds. It was time to make the magic happen. I was in the bathroom of that corporation for at least 30 minutes, checking my nails and nose and ensuring that I looked ready for the role. I showed up at the place an hour early because of the fear of traffic or an accident. Overkill? You could say that, but I wasn't going to allow anything to make me late. I had memorized my slide deck and my resume. KEY POINTER: You will be less nervous in your interview if you know your stuff. Questions about your resume— gaps in employment or short-tenured jobs—will come up, and you should be prepared to discuss them. Have an answer ready and move past those questions. Be confident and bold in your delivery. Have questions prepared about the company and be able to speak to your weaknesses. Preparation is required because you may only get this one shot for this company.

I had almost sweated through my shirt when they called me to the back. I kept saying to myself, "God has His Hands on me. I cannot fail." I shined in that interview! My presentation was great, and they stated that. My soon-to-be manager pushed a laptop to me and asked me to respond to a customer's complaint. I smiled because I knew they wanted to see if I could type. There, all those hours in prison, learning how to type kicked in. I responded to the email and made it look easy. They emailed me an offer letter the next day. *I repeat, learn how to type. Everything is IT now, so it will only help you going forward. It's helping me write this book you are reading or listening to. It's only clumsy when you first start but practice, and it'll be easy, quickly.*

The offer included full medical, dental, and vision packages, full benefits, and 36k a year, which is $17.34 an hour, plus the possibility of overtime. I had never made over $10 an hour, so this was a big jump, and I wanted it. Of course, in the fine print of the offer, it was contingent on a background check. My heart dropped, and reality slapped me in the face. I was so excited about how well I had done in the interview and the offer they sent me that I forgot that I was a felon and still on parole. I immediately checked myself in the mirror. This entire time, I told everyone that I was great and would do great things because God had His Hands on me, and I wouldn't fail. Yet, there I was, worried about a background check. *What can I say? I'm human, and we all have our fears that we fight daily. This was always one of mine.*

Most companies will do a background check, so mentally prepare for it. Yes, you may get turned down by certain companies because of their policies. It's ok. Most of us are turned down from time to time. That's that company's loss. They could have had a great employee, but a policy is a policy. While yes, you want this position, they also want you to fill it, so it works both ways. Sell yourself as an asset, and you will find that company that doesn't care about your past. To ease the shock, I typed out a two-page letter explaining everything in my background and what they might see when they ran the check. A background check doesn't provide many details, so I didn't want it to be black and white. The recruiter replied that they didn't go back beyond seven years and that the drug trafficking charge would not prevent me from getting the position. I got it.

Chapter 9
Let's Make Some Money

Making double what I had ever made and working all the overtime and holiday shifts I could get, it was time to find a better place to live. I was going through a divorce and custody battle, so I moved one block away from where my son's mother lived to make things easier for everyone. I wanted him to be able to go to the same school that he'd always gone to. We settled the divorce and had joint custody of my son, and things started to ease up. He and I lived in that apartment for several years until I bought my first house. I left the coffee shop and stopped being a student worker. With all the overtime that I was working, our lifestyle changed quickly. I had graduated from doing whatever I had to do to survive and working multiple jobs because I didn't have a choice. Well, we have choices now. I could spend the same hours I spent at the coffee shop and school at my new job and get paid a lot more. This was my first corporate position, and I embraced every aspect of it. I started to like this corporate world. No one other than that recruiter knew my background; to this day, no one in corporate America knows my background. They know the new me. This was just the beginning of my career. I always stated that if they allowed me to get my foot in the door, I would kick the door off its hinges. And did I ever.

Chapter 10
Good Times

I was asked to interview for a commercial for ITT Technical Institute. I was like, hell yes, let's do this. The school flew me to Miami Beach, Florida. I had always dreamed of going to Miami, but it just cost too much. The school paid for the entire trip. It was a same-day trip, so I didn't have a hotel, and I didn't pack anything. I just had on my favorite suit, my backpack, and a big ole smile. After the interview, I hung out on South Beach for the first time in my life. I had a couple of hours before my flight took off. My driver dropped me off and would pick me up when it was time to go to the airport. So, there I was, walking along the beach with my socks and shoes in hand and my pants rolled up. I'm sure most people looked at me as an idiot. But I was walking in the warm ocean, the sun shining and beautiful people all around me, so it didn't matter. I got a short set from a gift shop, balled that suit up in the bag, and was ready to hit the beach. I was like a kid in the water. This wasn't my first time to the ocean, but every time was like the first time for me. I love the ocean and the beach. I started picturing myself in a condo, overlooking the water with the fresh ocean breeze blowing through the windows. I knew the type of place that I wanted to move to. My forever home now would be in Miami. My plans were gaining clarity as I progressed.

Things were going great, and it was time to graduate. Unfortunately, I did get a B during my bachelor's degree. It was personal, and I tried to protest, but the dean wasn't listening. A's and B's were just as good, so why was I complaining? He didn't understand, and I didn't care at this point. It was time to walk that stage again. I graduated at the top of my class and was awarded the IT student of the year for Kansas and Missouri. My momma got to see me give my speech and receive my award. She was truly proud of me that day. That same plaque is hanging in my office today. I had the start of a great career, a bachelor's degree, and a nice place to live. Money was no issue because I was very frugal back then. I didn't party much. I was about school, work, and my children. I was single and happy. My biggest issue was my daughter's decision to live with her grandmother. I don't blame her today because I didn't utilize my time wisely and didn't invest in my daughter as I could have—something else that I get to live with.

Chapter 11
Corporate America

Keep in mind that I was only out of prison two and a half years before I accepted the offer with Savvis. Savvis is still the best company that I have ever worked with. I had great leadership and a cool manager. They truly cared about the employees and wanted to show their appreciation through food— free fountain drinks on every floor, Bagel Wednesday, and Chick-fil-A. I gained 60 pounds in three years at that company, and it felt good. I started at Tier 1 help desk. I had to answer phone calls, emails, and incident tickets. It was a lot of busy work, but we had fun with it. We had an awesome team, some that I am friends with. Should I say it again? I should've named this book *To This Day*.

I started to learn the ropes. I befriended the guy that everyone said was the best. I wanted to know what made him so good. He was eager to show me, and I ended up taking on more responsibilities within the team. This was in the first 90 days. I was starting to gain a reputation as one of the best, and management started to take notice. I joined the Champion team, which had nothing to do with IT. Hell, I liked the group's name, so that was enough for me. It was a way for me to get to know some of the company's leaders and show that I would go above and beyond. *You must do more than just your job to advance in any area. Everyone there is paid to do a job, but there are always those that stand out for the right reasons. Be part of that crowd, and you will advance quickly.*

I started to build friendships at the company. We had a lot of great people who were great in their own way. All our backgrounds were diverse, and that's what made it cool. We would take float trips and carpool to the Cardinals game and a few other trips. I was just one of the guys from work. I was guarded at first, but I relaxed when I felt how genuine everyone was. I was the designated driver on many of these trips, but I didn't mind because I was part of a team that hung out after work, had barbecues, invited me over, and so on. At this point, my childhood and prison friends were dwindling, and I needed to meet people I could hang out with that didn't default to talking about poverty. Yeah, we still talked about bull crap, but it wasn't violent and full of anger. I've been to several weddings and occasions because of this group. They all seemed to like me. None of them knew about my past, and I loved that. I have never been one to wear prison on my sleeves. I am an IT professional, and this was what we did to have fun. I started to embrace it more each day.

After I joined the Champion team, I started seeing a familiar face during most of our events. This was the same brother that would jump rope in the gym that we had on campus, and it would annoy the hell out of me. The gym was small, and he just had to do his rope jumping in the middle of everyone. Just rude, but bold also. So, I did some research. Who was this guy, and what was his title? I looked him up in the directory and discovered he was a director. Ok, now we need to meet officially. I scheduled a meeting on his calendar and asked if he would mentor me in corporate America. He accepted my offer, suggested a couple of books I should read, and asked me about golf.

To be honest, the only thing I knew about golf was Tiger Woods. He suggested I buy myself a used set of clubs and try it out because most successful men play golf, and a lot of networking happens because of golf. So, I jumped in with both feet. I had never swung a golf club, and my first time on the range was disastrous. I couldn't hit that ball to save my life! When I did hit it, it only went about ten feet. This was a lot harder than I had originally thought, but it was a challenge that I accepted. When I finally hit one of those balls the right way and watched it fly, I knew then that I had to have that feeling again.

My favorite engineer at Savvis happened to be a dedicated golfer, so we met at the range during lunch and after work to improve my swing and hit a bucket of balls. I finally squashed a ball again, and I was officially hooked. It felt so good to finally hit that damn ball from some distance and keep it straight. I fell in love with the game and played it as often as possible. Come to find out, many of the guys at work played golf. We had something else in common where we hung out, drank beers, and drove golf carts; we would occasionally smoke a nice cigar. *So, this is where my circle liked to play and let their guards down.* Those nine holes after a long day at the office can be therapeutic. I joined a golf league, and yes, I was the weakest link, but the guys didn't care. We would all spray that ball all over the place. Rich was the most consistent of the group. He had a nice swing. My mentor and I would play Forest Park often. He always won, and it didn't bother me at all. I just wanted to win more than one hole. I was starting to build my network of people that, had I not picked up that golf club, I probably would have never met. We plan golf trips to other states for the weekend sometimes. People are serious about golf.

The point of this story is to show you that you may need to step out of your element to achieve your goal. You can do it without golf, but ask yourself, is it worth spending $100 on some used clubs, with the reward of a new group of professionals to network with? I hope that your answer is yes. If it isn't golf, find something you like—chess club, book club, local gym, or something that will allow you to step out of your comfort zone and meet new people. This doesn't stop. It only increases with each level of success. Today, I have a golf group of great individuals, and we are creating a mastermind from this group. We have our logo and social media pages; STL Elite Golf Club, look us up. *Keep your mind open when it comes to learning new things. The old you will raise its head from time to time out of fear, but constantly check yourself and remind yourself of the goal. Stop holding yourself back!*

Chapter 12
First Project

A new project came about, and they asked for volunteers. I was the only team member who stepped up to the challenge. I mean, they would provide breakfast and pay me my hourly rate. This was a no-brainer for me. I just had to come into the office early. I was always the first in the office who made the first pot of coffee, so again, no brainer. That project continued for about three months and I was at my one-year mark. One of the rules of Savvis was that you had to remain in a position for a year before applying elsewhere in the company. I had been so happy with my position that I hadn't thought about the next one. I knew this $36,000 wasn't 100,000, so I needed to prepare for my next move. During this time, the sponsor of the project I volunteered for had flown in from the UK, and she said she wanted to meet me. I was puzzled because why did this lady want to meet me? I was just a Tier 1 help desk, and she was a senior director from another country. I met her for lunch, and she insisted on me drinking a beer if I wanted to. This was weird because we had to return to the office, and it didn't seem right to have a beer at lunch. She insisted, so I complied. I mean, she was my boss's boss's boss. She said she admired my passion for the project and the work I did to complete it ahead of time. She also stated that she liked how I dressed. Most of my peers wore shorts and t-shirts, but I always kept it GQ (good-looking). My motto: Mediocrity is a sin. I can't walk around her looking like the rest. I wanted to look like my next position, so I always kept a buttoned-up shirt and some slacks. I was shocked that she had noticed me. I thought it was cool as I finished my beer and free lunch.

A manager was preparing a slide deck for our new region in India, and she asked if she could use me as an example. I was dumbfounded. Why did she want to use me as an example? She stated that every time she saw me, I had a smile on my face. When things were rough, and they got rough at times, I kept a positive attitude. I wanted to tell her, "Lady, if you only knew where I have been, you would understand. I made the company newsletter that month, and I was proud of myself for a moment, but this Tier 1 position had run its course.

I remember my one-year review with the manager that hired me. He reminded me of the interview and said that he thought if I were anywhere near as good as I pitched myself, I would be worth hiring. He also said I surpassed everything he thought I would have done. I was shocked but not surprised. I was more shocked at the fact that he remembered my interview. Managers have interview's all the time, but he remembered mine. I've been to his house for pool parties several times. Jeff is still one of the coolest managers I ever reported to. He offered me a pay raise to stay on his team, but it was time for the next step of my career. He knew he couldn't keep me on the team because I had mentioned my goals and he believed that I would achieve those goals based on my work ethic and willingness to do what I needed to help the team—first to come, last to leave. I created the schedules for our rotation and held the team accountable when they were slacking. It was time to go. I started looking for my replacement.

With my responsibilities within the team, I needed someone strong who would take the torch. Big Bear was my guy. He had started helping with some of my responsibilities and had the grit I was looking for. It helped that he was 6'5", 350lbs, but he was barely old enough to buy liquor. Wet behind the ears, as we call it, but he had a brilliant mind and a passion for excellence, so he had my recommendation.

Chapter 13
Next Position

My next step was Tier 2 Help desk. This was the position that they had been grooming me for as I got closer to my first anniversary. One of my favorite managers approached me one day and asked me to apply for a position I had never heard of: Release Manager. Why would I apply for a Release Manager position? I didn't know any release managers at the company. She asked me to apply anyway, so I did.

I had to do some studying. What exactly is a release manager? I could only Google the role because it didn't exist within the company. Typically, I would reach out to someone in the role to get some insight. This was a new team and new role for the corporation, so I was on my own.

The interviewing process started, and I had a phone interview with two guys from the UK. I love their accents, and it was an easy interview. I thought, maybe this is a good position for me. It didn't exist within the company, and I could champion this role. The manager that asked me to apply mentioned that she had heard about how well I had done in the interview, and they were talking about me being a finalist for the position. I needed a presentation. My goal was to stand out from the rest, even if they had more experience. I worked on this presentation for two weeks leading up to the final interview. As I walked into the office for the interview, I saw the senior director from the UK, who had taken me to lunch and insisted that I drink a beer. She offered me the position over the other finalist with more than five years of experience. Later, I asked her why and she said she liked how I dressed and my passion for greatness.

The lessons in this are simple:

- Keep a positive attitude, no matter the task or position. You may never know who's watching or who's involved in what you are doing. Be great.
- Go above and beyond. Refuse to be mediocre. "Yeah, all the other workers are doing it and getting away with it. So, what?" You are on a mission that they are not.
- Volunteer. Get involved with the company. It's very hard to get noticed when you do what they hired you to do. You will be the first to get laid off.
- Always dress to impress. Most IT departments have no dress code. I've come to work and saw everyone wearing a ball cap on game day, with shorts and a t-shirt. My casual Fridays were the only day you would catch me in a polo. Plus, I look good in formal wear.
- Do your research. Make Google your friend. If there is something that you don't know about, it should only be because you haven't heard of it. If it's something that you deal with daily, do your research.
- Treat everyone with respect. You never know who may be the one hiring you next. The janitor, the line cooks, and the President/CEO should all know your first name. Be a presence no matter where you are or who you are around. Own the room.

Chapter 14
New Opportunity

I remained in this position for one and a half years and was making $46,000. The position started at $50,000, but because my salary was only $36,000, company policy wouldn't allow me to get that large a raise. I was happy with the $46,000—almost half the way to six figures. I got to meet some great people from overseas. Two managers from the UK got their first tour of the States, with me as the guide. The looks on their faces were like that of an adult child. They had never been to America, and their first time was with me. The things we take for granted, they don't, and it's great to get their perspective. I found it fascinating, and it changed my view of the world. I had to pass on an opportunity to travel to Europe because I was on parole and didn't have a passport. I do now, and there are a few stamps on it. I explained to my leadership that I couldn't go because of college. I wanted to go so bad!

I met a gentleman at Savvis from Pakistan, Abdul, aka Dulo. Great guy, by the way, and he opened my eyes to how the world saw Brown people and compared it to America. We had some fascinating conversations about world things, and there was never a dull moment. He is still one of my best friends to this day. He helped me see the value in purchasing a home and connected me with the realtor who would find me a home, my first home as an owner. *The point of this story is that you can meet some great people if you open your mind and not judge based on race, creed, or color*. Sometimes, we do it without thinking, and you could miss out on a lifelong friend. Being biracial, it was easy for me to embrace new cultures. You will learn that in technology corporations, most engineers are brown people. You'll hear a lot of new accents and embrace them. I thought that it was great to hear some of them speak. I would get personal candies from India each year, which were delightful.

As great as my team was, the annual raises were not enough to deal with inflation, much less progress in salary. I looked internal and saw a position I could do in my sleep, and it gave me the raise I wanted from my release manager role. I started looking internally for my replacement. There was an ongoing joke that no one could get Jerry to leave Tier 1. He had been there for over five years. I knew that I could teach Jerry because he was one of the best at Tier 1, and we respected each other. He listened to my guidance and applied for the position. With my recommendation, he was offered my old role. They almost put a plaque on the wall for me because I was the only one that could convince Jerry to take a new role and leave Tier 1 helpdesk.

My next role was as a Solution Delivery Coordinator. This move bumped my salary to $52,000. I was only there for a short span, but I loved the team. We would play poker together and fantasy football. We took a few float trips; if you have never taken a float trip, add it to your bucket list. You will thank me when we meet—if you go. Then, Savvis was bought by Centurylink, and life changed.

The new company started to make cuts. No longer did we have our fountain sodas, bagels, or Chick-fil-A. I decided to update my resume. I had been at Savvis for a little over three years. I hadn't thought about my resume because I loved this company and planned to be a director. This was no longer that company.

As soon as I updated my resume, the headhunters started calling. I was like, whoa. I had a few interviews, and nothing really jumped out at me. I had made it to the final round of interviewing for a contracting position with iBridge, where I would be working at Express Scripts as a release manager. I did my homework; the company had a horrible reputation for working their workers hard, long hours, and weekend shifts. It was considered a sweatshop. That didn't deter me because I was used to working a ton of overtime at Savvis, so let's see what this is all about. They made me a great offer that I couldn't refuse. *We'll discuss those details later.* Before I moved to the new company, I asked for some references.

A tactic of mine is to get letters of recommendation. When you work with someone and go above and beyond, ask for a letter of recommendation. If asked why, tell them you are building your portfolio. Some may ask you to write it yourself, and that's ok too. They will adjust it and sign off with their signature. ~~What you want is their signature.~~ This is the equivalent of a reference. The beauty in this is you have a signed document. That will aid you with your next position. Below is one that I received from Dan, my main man Wallace while at Savvis:

I am writing to recommend Ernest Moss for the position of Release Manager with your company. I have worked with Ernest

for the last 3 years and have been impressed with his tremendous abilities. The company we work at lacked a true Release Management group, and Ernest essentially built it from the ground up. I work as the Client Change Manager and know firsthand how Ernest's contributions to our company have positively affected many people and processes. Ernest took a job that had no blueprint to follow and ran with it. I was part of the rollout of this position and knew there were many candidates that applied. Before the interviews even started, a couple of the Senior Managers that have worked with Ernest were adamant about hiring him. The common theme was "Ernest is an exceptional worker that would be able to handle the task." Aside from knowing Ernest on a professional level, I have gotten to know Ernest on a personal level. He is the most positive person I know and considers no one a stranger. I have seen him in the break room, halls, and/or lunchroom, and everybody from the executive staff to the cleaning crew will make a point to speak with him. Everyone likes to surround themselves with positive people, and Ernest definitely fits this mold. He recently influenced me to go to graduate school to continue improving myself. As a matter of fact, we were speaking about it at lunch one day, and that evening, he emailed me a list of possible school programs I may be interested in. This small example defines Ernest. He didn't just simply listen to me speak about it. He went and researched various options, compiled them, and delivered them to me so I could make an informed decision.
The Senior Manager's assessment of Ernest was "spot on." Ernest is an exceptional worker and can handle any task.

This recommendation is still on my LinkedIn profile. I have a few, but this one stood out then and still stands out. You'll be surprised by the responses you get from your peers. They see you differently than you see yourself, and some remember things that you don't think about. *Something that you need to create if you haven't, is a LinkedIn account. You should only see postings from corporations, job leads and professional topics. Great articles are found there also. I received several offers from recruiters here, so please set it up and add this tool to your belt. It's free and easy to manage.*

Chapter 15
Master's Degree

Something I didn't mention; I had started my master's degree program at Lindenwood in Managing Information Technology. I missed school, and the company gave discounts to their employees, so it was an easy decision. The master's degree was easier than any of my degrees. I made straight A's and one B. Again, this B was personal, but I didn't make a fuss about it this time. I was making good money and close to getting off parole.

I thought about obtaining my doctorate, but I asked myself, do I really want to invest this amount of time and money for a degree, only for a title and bragging rights? I mean, it would be cool to have the title of Dr. Moss. Upon my research, a doctorate in information technology wouldn't yield me a salary much higher than I had, so I decided not to pursue this additional degree. Plus, the debt I had accrued was building because of these student loans. I had invested enough into my college career. I started looking at certifications. There are many in Technology. Some may say that you don't need a degree to have a career in information technology, and they are right. Two things can be true; you don't need a degree, but it only helps. You can pass a 90-day certification and get a job in information technology; this is also true. Both can get you a position in IT individually, but what could it get you if you had both degrees and certifications? I didn't want to limit myself to one or the other, so I got both. A friend of mine applied to a company and was turned down because he only had certifications, and this company only hired graduates. Tim is one of the smartest minds I know, but he didn't have the required credentials to get an interview. He had set limits to what and where he could apply because of having one over the other. He's still happy, so it's your call.

Degrees and certifications show that you have discipline and can pass a test. Some cultures study memorization techniques to help them pass tests and gain credentials. This doesn't mean they are more knowledgeable than the next person; they are often not. Yet, they continue to get top-paying jobs. It's how corporate America is designed. You will receive emails with titles that have a list of acronyms behind their name. In Corporate, this means you are someone of great importance and knowledge. The reality is that they are often the dumbest professionals that you will ever interact with, but they were smart enough to get the credentials needed to get their foot in the door. So dumb or smart? That's up to your interpretation. I will say that they make a lot of money because of those credentials.

Something major happened when I graduated with my master's degree. My brother, on my dad's side, came to my graduation. I only had a picture of him that my dad had given me on Christmas. I was four years old, and he was two years younger than me at the time. This was the last time I saw my dad alive. I resented my dad until he passed, and I didn't have many feelings to give to his death. But I always wanted to meet my brother. Facebook is a hell of an application because it links people from around the world, and I had found someone who could get me in contact with my little brother. He called me and said he would try to make it to my graduation. He came with his entire family. I thought walking the stage was a big deal but meeting my brother for the first time, there was no comparison. Yeah, I cried like a baby again. He was awesome and not in the streets. All my family up to this point was from the streets. He worked for the government and was relieved to know that I wasn't a loser like most of the family members. Both sides.

We have so much in common, and I make annual trips to Chicago to visit my little brother. Until then, I knew no one from my father's side of the family. I only knew my dad, who I didn't know, and my brother from a picture, but here he was at my graduation. The sad thing is that my brothers on my mother's side were not there. My other brothers have issues with drug addiction, something that I never had to struggle with. I don't know when hard drugs became cool to use, but they had it in their mind that this was the thing to do. I had to distance myself from all my brothers besides Michael, from my dad's side. We often talk about life and family—a lesson you will learn during your journey. Your family will no longer fit into your circle unless they are on a similar path. A Corporate IT worker doesn't have much in common with drug addicts. Our conversations were about past times and heartache and pain. I was never the family's favorite, so it wasn't a big deal to me. I was focused.

Chapter 16
Adjunct Instructor

I still visited ITT Tech. I liked talking to the students about what they could do if they applied themselves. The school had a bad reputation. I didn't agree with that and tried to change the minds of the new students. I was a success and that had a lot to do with my school. So, I volunteered to speak at one of the graduation ceremonies. It was great. The students were fired up, and the families were hyped. The IT chair of ITT Tech had lost a few instructors and asked me if I would teach. She literally dropped to her knees at the campus and asked me to teach for her. "Please get up off the ground. Of course, I will teach for you," I replied. She needed me to teach the next day, and I wasn't on the payroll. She and the dean stated that they would add to my check when I was hired. They had to vouch again, but I was hired, and now, I was an instructor at the same college I signed up for while in prison. Don't lose sight of the fact that I was still on parole. My dream was becoming a reality, and no one knew that I was a convict still on parole! The school didn't care. My actions and words spoke volumes compared to the issues I had in my past life. I liked that.

This wasn't a part of my plan at all. I never desired to teach until I was offered an IT adjunct instructor position. I thought, why the hell not? I knew my stuff, and I had a way with people. Plus, I cared about the students and wanted them to be successful. So, I wasn't the easiest instructor to deal with. I didn't tolerate late work and missing class; you would be guaranteed an F, and yes, I've passed out a few of those. My rules were simple: Show up and put forth an effort. Don't turn in late work, and you could pretty much expect an A. I wrote this out on the board on the first day. If anyone in the room didn't want to comply, I would not be offended if they did not waste their time or mine and got up and left. Some got up and left to change their class. I respected that honesty. I didn't want them to pay for a class they had no plans to complete. College is not cheap, so be honest with what you can do because many instructors could care less. You get what you earn and pay for. *So, if you are going to jump in with both feet, then do that. Wasting time is one of the biggest hurdles you will need to overcome if you plan to succeed.*

I didn't grade the students on knowledge because they were here to learn. I graded on effort and participation. I knew that if they showed up to class and did their labs and homework, they would learn and be smarter than when they started in my classroom. I would intentionally leave them in the lab, lost. I would go and hang out in the back offices and sip hot tea. The instructions were to tap your neighbor and ask if they had gotten past the issue you had. This annoyed some students because they were used to being told what to do and to call on the instructor when they ran into issues. Not in my class. I wanted them to learn how to talk to a peer before going to a manager for help. The answers are normally right next to you, but some have a default setting to ask the manager or instructor. This will not work in corporate America. They expect you to know something and, if you don't, to figure out what the issue is. When you go to your manager, you stop them from doing their job to help you with something that the person sitting next to you is a wizard at. That is a bad move for someone who's building their career. They still didn't like it, but they had no choice but to. The beauty of this is that they started to build friendships, and now, they know the names of their peers. *This aided me through college and within corporate America. But again, it's up to you and your level of commitment to your new career.*

I heard all the excuses. I was flirted with by a few of my students because they wanted a good grade. My integrity wouldn't allow me to fall weak. My reputation was impeccable, and no one would ruin that for me. Most of them dropped or stopped with the bullshit and got busy with their schoolwork—nice try, but right game, wrong player. I never crossed that line at any of the companies that I've worked for.

Most of my students confessed to me during their graduation, as I was straightening up their ties, that they hated me the first few weeks of class. I was too strict and straightforward. I seemed mean, but they discovered that that wasn't true. I required open and clear communication. If you were going to be late or miss a class or whatever, I needed to be informed. They also confessed that they learned more from my classes than all the others combined. I confessed to them, that was my goal as an instructor. *As a teacher, there is no better feeling than to know that you helped someone to become more knowledgeable and pursue their dreams.*

One of my favorite students had run into some spousal issues, and I was there for her as much as I could be during the time. I never toed the line with being unethical. It just wasn't my style, but she was a favorite, so we were more personal than the other students. She made her way out of that bad situation and was engaged. I was so proud of her, and I liked her new guy. If he was anything like he portrayed, he would be a good one. To my surprise, she asked me to give her away to her husband. I was flattered, to say the least, but I agreed with no hesitation. Plus, the wedding was on a beach in Miami? I want parts of all that smoke. It felt weird being the oldest person again and being called 'Mr.' or 'Professor' during the celebration, but it was an honor to be referred to by a title. This same student has a son with her new husband, and I am the godfather. We remain closer than my blood relatives, and there's nothing like seeing my little guy smile when he sees me. *To know a lot of what they have been through and continue to deal with is a testimony to what love can conquer and what dedication can build. Saying that I am proud of her does it no justice.*

You all have heard that there isn't much money in teaching, and you heard right. Teachers are maybe the most underpaid of all the careers. I didn't make much as an instructor, but it kept me sharp on my knowledge and added another slot to my resume. Plus, the joy I received when my students landed that first job or got their first promotion. That made it all worth it to me. My hourly salary was only $28 an hour, and I normally would work two classes a week. There's something about looking at a resume and seeing someone who teaches IT; it's impressive and eliminates many general questions they ask during interviews.

I mentioned this little nugget because I want you all to know that you can do whatever your heart desires, but you must practice integrity. The leaders of the school knew, as a student who never missed a class and always had a smile that I greeted everyone with, that I would be a great instructor, and I was. I pretty much grew into my career because of that school, but that school would have been just another debt and waste of my time had I not applied myself. Look online; you'll see the hate for ITT Technical Institute and other colleges. Don't allow that to persuade you. College works if you work it. If you expect to be given a degree without work, then you should expect a career with limited opportunities.

Chapter 17
My Offer

As I normally do, I killed the iBridge interview. They contacted me the next day with an offer. As a contractor, I was offered $95,000 a year, with the possibility of overtime. Going from a full-time salary position to a contractor can seem risky. Being a contractor, you don't get much in benefits, and if you are fired, there is no unemployment. You must pay a premium for your health insurance. Thank God for the Affordable Care Act (Obama Care). High risk, high reward. I turned in my two weeks' notice the next day. I remember my manager at the time saying that I would be a fool to turn that offer down, even as a contractor. Centurylink was upsetting everyone, and they had made us all fully vested with our 401k, so it was easy to leave.

The hardest part of it all was leaving my peers. We had developed a strong bond during our time at Savvis. They all wanted to know how to get a position paying them $95,000. iBridge mentioned that for every employee they hired that was referred by me, I would make a dollar an hour for every hour they worked. At least ten people left Centurylink to work for iBridge because of me. They all were given close to double their pay. It was so bad that the security department at Centurylink blocked any emails with iBridge listed in the text. I was trying to bring all my friends with me. We still laugh about it, and they will still thank me for helping them to get their next opportunity. Some of their wives and mothers thanked me at events. It wasn't only because of me. I knew that these guys were rockstars that had gotten complacent. Some of those guys are vice presidents and directors today, and I can call on each of them for references or talk.

A position opened on my team for a backup release engineer. The guy who trained me had taken another role, and now, I was able to move up and assist with hiring someone new. I had just the guy in mind. Darrin shadowed me at Savvis while he was still in college. We developed a bond and kept it going for years. It's still going. What I loved about Darrin was that he was teachable while being smart as hell—one of the smartest guys I've met in corporate America. When I left Savvis, he was on the Solution Delivery team and was a rockstar. If I had a choice, Darrin would be my backup. His only issue was being young without a lot of experience. That didn't bother me at all. It did concern my manager, but she took my word for it and hired him.

Darrin was all in and picked up what we were doing quickly. I had no doubts. We put in a lot of hours at Express Scripts and we developed a stronger bond. His family would thank me every time I came to his place for a gathering. His salary was doubled because of my referral, and his family was grateful for that. To be clear, Darrin had to do his part in the interview and take the step from being a full-time employee to a contractor, so it wasn't all because of me. He deserves plenty of credit because he trusted my guidance and wasn't afraid to take his next step. *There's a power in alignment.* He and I aligned on most things, and when we didn't, we respected each other enough not to allow anything to break our bond. In the same way the senior director saw something in me, I saw it in him and took a chance on someone with no release management experience because I knew the work ethic and the character.

Express Scripts was going through a merger and acquisition of another company in New Jersey, which impacted our team. A year into the new position, I was becoming the badass I am, and the company was starting to take notice. I convinced my manager to allow me to fly to New Jersey and train the new team on how the release management team handled releases, whether scheduled or off cycle. She agreed, and I was able to bring Darrin with me.

The company had a private jet, and we were going to New Jersey with the leadership team as contractors. Never in my wildest dreams did I imagine this. A convict, on parole, flying on a private jet? I didn't know anyone who had flown on a private jet. It was everything that you could imagine. We didn't have to go through airport security and take our shoes off. We walked right into the jet from a shuttle bus from the company. We were greeted with beer, wine, and steak sandwiches. Darrin and I looked at each other like, "Wtf?" We looked at our manager, and she said it was ok to have a beer or a glass of wine. This was during the day and while we were on the clock. This is the second time that this has happened to me. Maybe my thoughts on corporate America were reserved.

As Darrin and I were waiting for the shuttle to the newly acquired company, we both thought it would be nice to be driven to work in this stretched Mercedes Benz that we were staring at in front of the hotel, and you know what happened. Our driver showed up and escorted us to the company in that Benz. This was nice and another first for me. We met a lot of people and had a great time. The director treated us to a day in New York—another first for me. New York was always a destination on my bucket list, and I got to experience it free of charge. After looking at the dinner bill for six people, it had to be on the company's tab because it exceeded $3000. That's high, but it was the best steak that I've ever eaten in my lifetime. Times Square was as advertised—so many eateries and characters on the street. I felt like a kid that had finally left the porch.

Guess what? I had made it to six figures after being out of prison for less than six years while still on parole, and I had flown on a private jet. With the additional $1 an hour and the overtime I charged at Express Scripts, I was winning, and no one could tell me anything. I couldn't wait to show my family, which was a mistake because now they had their hands out, and those that didn't had a frown. You may think that everyone wants you to succeed, but many don't. Your success can be a slap in their faces because of dumb reasons. Be careful with who you communicate your wins. Your circle will be more supportive than your family, and the circle doesn't expect anything from you. But family will. My goal had been reached. It was time to create a new goal: What steps do I need to take to increase my salary to $150,000? If you want to break this down to an hourly rate, we are talking $75 an hour. I was making $50 an hour, and it just wasn't enough to satisfy me at this point.

Chapter 18
Step Back

You may say it's greedy, but $50 an hour still wasn't enough. I wanted more. I had gotten to this point sooner than I had thought, and now, I wanted to take my salary to another level. My master's degree was the last degree I would obtain. The market stated that those with a PMP (Project Management Professional) certification could make a higher salary. So, while I was happy with my six figures, I started preparing myself for the next role. The PMP was and still is the hardest test I ever passed—I failed it twice. Some IT positions require that you have certain certifications, and the PMP was by far the most recognized in the industry.

I was asked to speak at a conference on a college campus, and I bumped into a peer with whom I had taught. He was focused on construction but was corporate through and through. We both presented to the students and answered questions. We exchanged information but never followed through with any communications. We met up again at a cigar lounge. I was meeting a date, which turned out to be a dud, and here came Vince. *Now how do I keep running into this dude?!* He enjoyed a good cigar and loved golf. We taught in the same building for years and never had an in-depth conversation before now. It was mainly about suits and looking nice at the school. Come to find out, Vince was dealing with the same corporate issues in construction that we deal with in technology. He had a golf group that met him at the cigar lounge, and we all sat and chatted. I'm currently a member of the golf group, and we have polo shirts with the name of our group now. We hang out and exchange ideas over a nice stick and a cup of whiskey from time to time, and we are friends to this day! *Remember, when someone continues to show up in your activities leading to your goal, embrace them. Start a conversation. This could be the person assigned to your journey that could fast-track your goals and career.*

While studying for my PMP, I continued asking my manager to convert me from a contractor to a full-time employee, and each time, I was met with excuses. This is not rare for contractors. Large organizations are only allotted several full-time employees compared to contractors. This saves the company the risk of paying you benefits and health insurance. Yes, you make more money, but you sacrifice the extras. So, I updated my resume and now accepted an offer with an initial salary of $115,000 a year. I had changed jobs to be a project manager at a hospital's IT department and looked to continue to grow my career.

Unfortunately, the budget was cut for the IT department, and I was let go. I went from making $115,000 a year to being unemployed. I still had my instructor position, but teachers don't get paid what they are worth. I had handled my finances well up to this point, but I was a year into my first house that I had purchased, and now, I only had a part-time job as an adjunct instructor. Remember, there is no unemployment being a contractor. This just gave me more time to study for my PMP. I had money from months saved up for days just like this.

Chapter 19
PMI

My career was starting to shift. I was always designated the project manager in my classes where we had projects. At first, I was like, "Wait, I want to do the engineering work too." They knew one thing: I would make sure that we hit each deliverable within the project and that everyone would be held accountable for their part. I didn't play about my grades, and no one would slack off and cause me to get a B. My teammates knew this well, so they wanted me to manage the project. This caused me to start thinking about becoming a project manager, but I knew you needed a ton of experience and credentials. I had the skills, but I didn't know what all this role entailed. I started to do my RESEARCH.

I joined the local PMI (Project Management Institute) chapter. Again, I knew no one in the room, and there were at least 100 professionals networking. So many different cultures and ethnicities; this is awesome, I thought. Each company in the St Louis area was represented in this room. *One thing you will learn in corporate America is that employees get referral bonuses when they refer and you are hired.* All that I needed was to show them who I was and where I planned to go with my career. They were lining up to recruit me for their companies. I volunteered at PMI for many years and moved up. I was the director of corporate outreach. I must be honest; I wanted the title. I had no clue what a director of corporate outreach did, but I was willing to learn. My

VP was Zeke, and I will say that he had a presence about himself and a commendable calmness. We dealt with many tough conversations, but Zeke was always the voice of reason and a true leader of people. He taught me a ton, and eventually, I became the vice president of Outreach, and I had three directors that reported to me. We took annual trips to different states, and the networking opportunities were abundant. I was also studying for the PMP, and now I was on the board of directors of the group that wrote the PMP. Nothing but greatness could spring from this. My circle was starting to grow by the day.

I passed the PMP the same week I accepted a new position with Enterprise Holdings as a support manager. They offered me $95,000 a year, and I negotiated it up to $100,000 yearly, with full benefits. A contractor making $100,000 a year is a lot different from a full-time employee making $100,000 a year. I had found my home company and stopped looking for other positions. This was the one that I had been waiting for. I was unemployed for four months. I had offers, but none met my criteria. My networking circle regularly sent me job opportunities, but each had flaws— either the money wasn't right, or it was something I didn't want to do. I wanted to be able to work from home if I decided to. I was not going to settle for less than six figures. I was done settling. During those four months, I did have to sell my truck, but it was worth it. I have a much better truck now.

There will come times when you will need to make hard decisions. Just make sure that they align with your plan and your goals. It wasn't hard for me to sell a few things to make ends meet. Don't get too attached to material things because they come and go. What you think is nice right now will soon become nothing as you progress. You'll find yourself laughing at what you held high as having the most value. It's nothing.

Chapter 20
Parole

I was still on parole during this time. I had no violations or encounters with law enforcement. I was squeaky clean, and they wouldn't let me off parole a day early. Normally, you get off a few months early for good behavior. Not me. When I would mention this to my parole officer, he would try to convince me to speak to some of his clients, and I refused each time. I didn't want to endorse the probation and parole office. They had helped me none. I did this on my own, with the help of some loved ones and great friends. I told him I had a goal that didn't involve the parole office. However, I was going to give back and help some of those that may relate to what I've been through. I was going to do that on my own, in a grand fashion.

For clarification, I am not anti-parole board. I had a home and a support system, so I didn't need their assistance. A parole officer will have a list of resources for those that need them—job leads, housing assistance information, and so on. If you are struggling in any of those areas, ask them about it. That's part of their job, and most POs will gladly help those who want to be helped, but you must use your WORDS if you expect anything to happen. One thing that will take you a long way is to check your attitude at the door. Parole officers have a job to do, and the last person they want to deal with is someone with a piss poor attitude. It works both ways; you may have a PO with a shitty attitude. So, what? You are here to fulfill your parole obligations. Greet that person with a smile, a check stub, and a bladder ready to take a urinalysis test. Offer to take the urinalysis test. It just keeps a record of you being clean. When you do this, you limit the conversation. You can control the conversation by coming to them prepared to talk about college or the job or your next certification. Your energy will be felt, and you shouldn't have a lot of issues with your PO. They have enough of the dumb dumbs to deal with.

I had been released from prison on 6/07, and it was 12/14, my last month on parole. The weight had been a lot to bare, but I did it. Were there bad times? Of course. But my worst day free is better than my best day incarcerated. *It will get tough, and you may feel weak, but how you deal with that will determine how successful you are.* There were plenty of opportunities for me to go back to prison. You all don't understand the bullshit that I went through that I didn't include in this book. I didn't because that wasn't important to me, and it shouldn't be important to you. Just know that you are going to go through some things. Just keep going because you are driven by belief and guided by a plan. Your words should speak life into your journey, not death, so be careful of what you say. WORDS mean stuff. I promised my mom and children I would never return to prison. Not only had I not gone back, but I had also walked down my parole with no violations. I could honestly say for the first time in my life that I was a law-abiding citizen. I wanted to celebrate in a major way, and now, it was time to get a passport and see another country.

While on parole, you are not allowed a passport unless the rules have changed. I was excited to know that I could leave the country if I wanted to. A sense of freedom comes when you open that mail and see your passport picture. I took my first cruise, a three-day Bahama cruise. Just seeing the water and Caribbean colors is worth the trip. The food was amazing, and the staff treated me pretty well. Then I stayed in a five-star resort in Punta Cana. My life changed and for the first time in my life, not only did I feel like a king, but I was being treated like one.

You are treated differently when you visit a five-star resort. They are trained to cater to your every need. This was a new experience for me. I cried like a baby on the beach. The group I was with didn't understand, nor did the person I was with. I wasn't trying to make them understand either. My entire life came out that day, and I found peace with many things I had been holding on to that served me no good. My entire outlook on life changed during that trip. I stopped feeling like a convicted felon. I felt free for the first time in my life. *If you are on parole or probation or have never had the means to visit another country, plan for it. Treat yourself to finer things, and you will start to expect finer things. After going through what we've been through, we deserve a trip out of the country. Another of my regrets; I didn't enjoy life as I should have during my transition. Yes, there were plenty of good times, but I never treated myself for all the hard work I had put in to get to this point. When time is gone, there's no getting it back. We can always make more money, but time is limited and should be maximized.*

Chapter 21
New Start

Still working as an Instructor at ITT Tech, I was no longer a contractor making six figures. I was a full-time employee with benefits and inexpensive health insurance. I had a nice cubicle in a great location. I awarded myself with a Jaguar, Van Den Pas. My kitty kat. I also purchased my first investment home, and I graduated with my master's degree. I didn't have to worry about bills anymore. I made more than enough to cover them all with my salary from Enterprise. My days of hustling were in the past.

I was a salaried worker again, and there's comfort in knowing that your checks will be the same each payday. No more working crazy overtime and late nights. I had graduated to a position of trust and started with a company that stressed work-life balance. I didn't know what to do with all my free time. The college closed permanently, so my teaching side job was gone. I found myself making more money than ever, but I was bored after work. PMI only met once a week and had a monthly dinner. Enterprise was going great. I started networking and meeting some more great people. Some of my friends had accepted positions at Enterprise also. We were calling it Savvis East.

I was hired as a support manager. I did have to work some weekends when we had releases, but I was allowed to take an afternoon off from time to time to make up for that weekend work—totally different than what I was used to, and I liked it. It was by far one of the easiest jobs I've ever done. I was so used to Express Scripts, where you had to hustle, that this seemed slow. One lady I worked with at Express Scripts, and we were both now at Enterprise, told me to be prepared to be bored. She was telling the truth. I networked with people about everything but work; it was where I was most of the time. I even convinced a couple of friends to get their PMP and to get involved with the local chapter. They joined me at a couple of the dinners, which was cool. They both passed their PMP and started a study group for other peers interested in passing their PMP. You are probably smiling because you know exactly who I am talking about.

I started playing more golf and joined the Enterprise golf league, where I met some more cool people. I started to notice my physical health; wasn't good. I had gotten fat, fast. My doctor diagnosed me with diabetes. I had gained a lot of weight and was now 320lbs. *Working in corporate can do that to you, so be aware of your health. This isn't a story about my health issues, but I want to call it out as a warning or something to be aware of.* I should start working out with all this free time, I thought. I wasn't happy at home, so I didn't want to be there unless my son was with me— another story I will spare you all from for now. I hit the gym hard. I became obsessed with working out. I still am. Long story short, I lost 80lbs of fat, and I am no longer on any medication.

One of my first strategic moves at Enterprise was to meet the leadership team, not my manager but the higher-ups or big wigs. I had heard my VP on calls, and he seemed like a tough guy. He had a way with words that caused a lot of people to be intimidated by the sound of his voice. I was intrigued and wanted to meet him. So, I scheduled a meeting and sent him an invite. His administrative assistant informed me that I was not allowed to schedule a meeting with the vice president, but she would check his schedule and get back to me. I reached out to her after three months and asked for an update. She scheduled a meeting for he and I to meet.

My manager at the time was baffled. She didn't understand why I would want to meet him. No one liked him within my department, but I wanted to ask him about his leadership practices and more. Of course, he was late for the meeting—typical of leadership. I just sat there and observed his pictures and plaques on the wall. When he finally arrived at the meeting, he looked confused. He had no clue why I wanted to meet with him. It was simple; I wanted to know what he expected and desired from his leaders. I was new to the company and desired to move up within the leadership team, so I wanted to talk to the top dog. He laughed and said, "I wish there were more like you." His demeanor changed immediately. Now he was relaxed, and we chatted about a lot of things. From that moment when he saw me in the office, he would always stop by and ask me how things were going. My peers would look with mouths wide open. He didn't seem nice to many, but they saw him be nice to me. I was proud of that relationship.

Still bored at the new company, I joined the Diversity group. I love diversity, and it just made sense being biracial. Plus, I could meet some people within the company that was outside of the team. Within two weeks of joining, I was asked to be the group's chairperson. The original chairperson was leaving the company, and no one wanted to step up, so I decided I would. We had a ton of fun, and I met many great people who had a passion for diversity. We organized an event where all the represented cultures brought in their favorite dishes and passed out samples. I tried a lot of new and different foods, which were good. We had other events that were a success, but this was the one that I remembered the most. With all my free time, I thought about getting some training and seeing if the company would pay for it.

My department manager was an awesome guy. He took a liking to me. He loved my passion and freedom to speak to any audience. We developed a strong bond that my manager was not too keen about. I didn't care. Hell, I was cool with her boss, so what would she say to me? Yes, I had gotten a little arrogant by this time, and I didn't care about my manager anyway. She was the definition of a micromanager. *Be careful because that almost got me fired*, but my department manager had a big project coming, and he wanted me to champion it. Agile.

ag·ile

1. able to move quickly and easily.

2. relating to or denoting a method of project management, used especially for software development, that is characterized by the division of tasks into short phases of work and frequent reassessment and adaptation of plans.

I was clueless as to how that word fits with information technology. So, I needed to do some research. Through my research, I learned that the company had money allocated to professional growth and training, so I signed up for Agile training, and the company paid for it. They funded two of my certifications in Agile. *Always do your research within each company because they have a lot of money for training which is rarely used yearly.* You must go looking for it. I told all my peers about this, and most didn't know. For the two I mentioned earlier who passed their PMP at Enterprise, the company paid for the training and the cost of the test; it's not cheap. Google it. *The beauty of these certificates is that you take them with you. If you leave the company for any reason, you are now certified in additional areas of expertise, which adds to your marketability. Strategically think when you are building your career. No job is promised to you. Cuts always happen in corporate America, so to prepare yourself for that, continue to build your resume and portfolio.*

Ok, I had my certifications and my objective. There is a saying in corporate America, "Don't reinvent the wheel." I started to do more research online and within the company. A couple of teams had adapted the Agile mindset and principles, so I wanted to check with them and see how things were going. Mr. Ray was my go-to person. He was someone I hadn't had many interactions with because of his walk and his clothes. It sounds funny saying that now, but the brother had a different type of swag, and I wasn't sure it aligned with me. Selfish as that sounds and judgmental as it is, it kept me distant. Upon further investigation, Mr. Ray and I had more in common than I knew or thought. We both enjoyed golf, investments, and more. I was wrong. *Never allow your judgment of someone within corporate America to be based on appearance. You will meet a lot of different personalities, races, and cultures. Embrace the difference because it will only aid in your growth. If I had kept my judgment of him, meeting my objective would have been extremely hard. Thank you again, sir!*

His team was going through the transformation from waterfall to Agile. Waterfall is the method of project management from where the PMP is written, similar in only a few areas. This was a great effort as it required a shift in mindset. I borrowed the flow chart his team had created and edited it to fit my objective and team. *Don't reinvent the wheel.* It was perfect, and I presented it to my department manager. He was in with both feet. I then needed to convince the management team to buy into the new mindset and process. They pushed back initially.

Agile will not solve your problems but will shine a light on them. We noticed that the management teams' default was to micromanage. This is frowned upon in the Agile world, but my department manager was endorsing this shift, and since they all reported to him, they had to comply. The engineers loved it! They were allowed to do their work without management telling them what and how to do it. "It doesn't make sense to hire smart people and then tell them what to do; we hire smart people so they can tell us what to do." -Steve Jobs. I added that quote to my emails and management saw it as a slap in the face, and I must admit, it was.

The movement was underway. My team (Dream team) was full of rockstars, to the point that the others in the department were jealous, and management eventually split our team and moved my engineers to the other teams. This happened as my department manager took another position with a different company. Now here I was, alone, and all the managers were pissed at me, and my support had left the company. They labeled me anti-management and almost put me on a behavior plan, which is not good. My new manager stopped the behavior plan. She came to our department in the nick of time because I would have left Enterprise had they put me on that plan, and that would've burned that bridge to the ground. I dialed back my harshness of micromanagement and started to coast again. By now, my job was second nature. I could do it in my sleep. I needed a new opportunity and started applying internally. I was denied each time and didn't understand why. I came to find out that I was getting negative feedback from the managers, and for those that know, that's not a good thing.

Not all the managers were micromanagers. I was in a department meeting and heard someone speak that caught my attention. He had commanding energy about him while knowing his stuff. I had heard him on some conference calls, but we had never met until this day. As I normally did, I approached him and started a conversation. I wanted to know how he felt about the Agile movement. His response was shocking as this was our first conversation, but he told me to rethink my approach. I told him I wanted to hear more. He continued and stated that while what I was doing was right and factual, how I delivered the message could improve, and the negative responses would change some. I was ready to defend my approach, but he cut me off and continued. "I'm not trying to tell you how to do your thing, but if you want a different outcome from the managers, the delivery needs to be adjusted," he said. He left it at that, and we had to return to work. His truths rattled my entire foundation, so I started rethinking my delivery because I was hiding behind the facts and being an asshole because I could.

I really didn't care for most of our management team, and I was deliberately being a jerk when I should have been more thoughtful about the drastic changes they were going through. It took Big Kimbo to put me in my place that day and alter my thinking. We started communicating more and hanging out. I would pose questions to him just to see where his thinking was because I respected his mindset and embraced the difference. He built his career in the financial side of corporate America, and over there, they are more buttoned up and polished, not so much in IT. I started leaning on him for mentorship and still do to this day. This is my brother from another mother, and we are bonded for life, all because of a conversation.

I started to soften my approach to management. I removed my Steve Jobs quote from my email signature and started to embrace my new manager. I liked her and her approach to our roles within the company. I was close to my five-year mark and salaried at roughly $120,000 with full benefits and profit sharing. After five and a half years, I was fully vested with my 401K, meaning that if I changed jobs, I would get all they had matched within those five years. *Most corporate professionals know these dates, and they plan for them.* If you are happy and your salary is decent, you can stay for five years and get all your money before you start looking elsewhere. Staying faithful to a company will keep you underpaid but with great benefits, additional vacation and more. So, it's up to you. I'm a capitalist, so I always go for the additional money, but it must be a significant amount to strike my attention. Plus, I'm in my forties, so there are only so many more jumps that I plan to make.

Unfortunately, my son's mother passed from cancer. I knew she had some serious issues, but I didn't know it was that serious. I was knocked back, and then I thought of my son. What could my little guy be thinking and feeling with all of this? I was devastated for him. My mom also had a round of cancer but made it through that first bout. Seeing her go through that is enough to soften anyone. Cancer is just nasty. My son had lost a grandmother and now his mom to cancer, while his other grandmother fought the beast too.

One thing his mother knew was that I would take care of our baby boy. With all that she and I went through, she always knew what type of dad I was and that I would never turn my back on him. I never have, and I never will. He is my namesake, and he will be part of this legacy. I believe in nepotism. If it were all up to me, my entire family would be part of this legacy, but that's just not realistic with some of my family members. Things at home were not getting any better, and with the death of my son's mother, it just got worse, and I found myself in another nasty divorce. This being the worse of the two, easy. I felt horrible for my son because this was the closest thing to a mom he had left. But he had a dad, and we became closer. We were developing a partnership because he took care of me like I took care of him. I moved back to the neighborhood where he had gone to school his entire life because he wanted to finish with his friends—no problem.

I met the love of my life almost immediately after I wrapped up an ugly divorce. I sold my first home and had my son back in his school district. Life was starting to look up, and then COVID-19 happened, and the world paused for a long moment. In corporate America, everyone started to become nervous about their jobs. Layoffs were coming, and we all were wondering who would get laid off or let go. My main concern was that management would love to get rid of me after what we had been through, but other than that, I felt secure with my position. Plus, no one did the releases for my team but me, which was critical.

We were deemed essential workers because we provided rental vehicles for the COVID-19 nurses, doctors, and patients. My team was Payment Services, so they kept us employed to keep the payment processing for the most part. Layoffs came in two waves. Many of my friends were laid off and given severance packages, which I heard, were nice. They reduced IT by 25% after the second wave, and I made it through both. Being a full-time work-from-home employee, I didn't feel the sting many felt during COVID-19. My salary was reduced by 5%, but they took care of that once the world opened again, plus it saved me in taxes. The company was never the same to me. A lot of my friends had been let go, and it felt weird. I used to think that I would retire from Enterprise. Not any longer.

The manager I liked had taken another role as a department manager with a different team. Well damn! I didn't see that one coming, and now the question was, who would become my manager after she left? It was quickly announced that my original manager was becoming my manager again. Isn't that just wonderful? She was different this time. I think our history forced us to respect each other, and we didn't have any major differences going forward. COVID-19 softened up the world. People started to appreciate life and living. Many of my colleagues lost loved ones to the virus, and we all knew someone close that was impacted. It was scary back then, but we got through it and appreciated each other more. I lost the closest person to a dad I had ever known during the COVID-19 mess. I never called any man dad, but I called Kenny "pops" and looked up to him all my young life. *Sometimes, the best ones leave us too soon. Cherish your loved ones and check on them. Covid should have taught all of us that.*

I was getting bored with my role, so I started looking outside the department and the company for opportunities. Yes, I made good money and had a good job, but I wasn't stimulated anymore. I wanted a new challenge. I noticed that a project manager role became available, and guess which department? The same one that the manager that I liked moved to. Yes, this was financially a lateral move, but it was a move to something new, so I applied. I won't allege that my previous manager helped me in getting this new role, but I'm sure she played her part. She knew my work ethic and success rate. I accepted that position with the thought that I could advance my career in a new department. And there were a few familiar faces that I enjoyed working with. It was an easy decision.

Chapter 22

Last Ride with Enterprise

This new role was nice. I liked the team and met some really nice people in that department. My son was doing better at home and school. I married the love of my life and started viewing my life differently. I wanted more than just six figures. I wanted to start helping people again. We were doing well financially. A lot of trips and fine dining, something I had dabbled in on occasions, but my wife expected it, and I loved that. She has elevated me to mental and emotional heights that I never knew existed. I could write a book about the love of my life, and I just might.

As I stated, things were going great with all the changes. I was a happy man again. Then the worse happened; my mom lost her fight with cancer. She asked me to let her go, and I still haven't. She gave me that extra kick in the ass and a soothing touch when I needed it. My number one fan had moved on, and my world fell apart. Well, it almost did. My wife, children, and friends supported me through that time, and they still support me when I am weak. It's a hard pill to swallow when you lose your mom. My son was stronger than I was. He kept checking on me when he had lost both grandmas and his mom to cancer. He was checking on me! I cried for a long time every day, and I catch myself today crying for my momma, wishing she was still here to see her oldest strive and become a better person each day.

I will say this: Enterprise did great by me at the loss of my mom. Being salaried, I took off several weeks with pay, and they checked on me often. So much love was received from my colleagues at Enterprise, and that will never be forgotten. During this time, most of my extended family turned on me. My mom was the rock that kept us all together, and with her no longer there, all hell broke loose. I haven't spoken to some of my family since she left. Still, life must go on.

A year into this new role, I was ready to move on. Again, it wasn't the same after COVID-19. So, I started looking outside of the company and found a role paying me 30% more a year, but I would be a contractor again, not a full-time employee. My wife was a retired RN. She took a job to ensure that our family has the best insurance and benefits. So we agreed, and I accepted the new position with Charter. I turned in my letter of resignation. The department manager was unhappy with that decision, and sadly, I never heard from her again—no farewells, no congratulations, nothing. Some of the others in the department were sad to see me leave, but we are in contact sometimes.

Chapter 23
Final Corporate Role

I'll never accept another role with Charter! After I completed my exit interview and sent my laptop and equipment back to Enterprise, Charter mentioned that they had rescinded the offer and gave it to someone internal. WTH! The contracting company couldn't believe that they had done this because it was a first, and I suspect that someone heard about that position and blocked me from getting it after I resigned. I have no proof, but I feel it in my gut. Oh, and let's make matters worse, they called me on my birthday with the news that I was now unemployed.

Wow, this is one heck of a year, I thought. I lose my mom and pops, the family turns on me, and I'm unemployed for the first time in over six years. I had to pause for clarity because this was not making any sense. I wanted to burn some sage or something. One rough patch after another. Three teenagers in the house, all going through different stages of growth and maturity, and I'm out of work. Then something else crazy happened; my daughter's mother passed from cancer! Both of my biological children and I had lost our moms to cancer within five years. All different forms, but all are still cancer related. I wouldn't wish that on anyone. Yes, I'll agree that dads are important. I was raised mostly by a single mother, so forgive me if I lean that way in my thoughts. *Through these tragedies, my children and I are closer. Soon we will launch a company that supports people living with cancer and keeps our moms' legacies still going.*

89

I knew I was marketable, so I wasn't concerned with landing a new role. But why were all of these things happening to me, all within a year? I've never been one to believe in luck or happenstance. Everything happens for a reason, and something wasn't aligning within me, but I couldn't put my finger on it. I was getting burned out with corporate America. My greater calling continued to rise in my thoughts, and opportunities started to reveal themselves. I was getting offers from a lot of recruiters, but nothing was causing me to be excited. I took a role with Climate, making the highest 6 figures thus far and yes, as always, the team was great. I met many great people, but my heart wasn't in it anymore. I milked that salary for a few months and eventually left corporate America. Great ride. I could talk about even more stories, but they could be considered too graphic for this audience.

Corporate America was my first business partner. Because of the salaries I made over the past 13 years, I have been able to live a nice life, purchase several investment properties, and see many countries.

My purpose on this earth is to remain a success story and inspire those who have been in the trenches like I have.

Corporate America, my time is up.

Conclusion

This book aims to inspire and motivate anyone who wants to start over, and if a wreck like me could do it, you can too. This is a success story and is based on facts and events that happened during my journey. Take these steps and guidelines and get your six figures. Don't accept anything less of yourself. Doubt has no place in the mind of the successful. Control your circle or those who have access to you. If they are not with you, then they are against you or just in the way. I've lost many of my childhood friends through this process, and yes, sometimes the memories will flare up, and you may feel lonely. That's understandable, so prepare for it. Know that when it flares up, it is time to go back to your plan and habits and remind yourself why you are making this change. I stopped talking to many of my family members because they are who they are, which doesn't fit in my life. Selfish? Probably so. Family and friends can hold you back. And if you allow that, then expect what you have always gotten.

It's fine. Success is not for everyone. Some just like to exist and measure their life against those who don't have much.

Oh yeah, you are, 'winning, winning' in that case.

Lets discuss this online @themossmagic on IG or FB.

Thank you to all my readers and listeners. You all are the awesome ones who gave me some of your time to listen to a portion of my story. So much was left out, but we will talk more. I promise!